I Am Different by Design!

Cloresa Porter

Copyright © 2016 Cloresa Porter

All rights reserved.

ISBN:0692729526
ISBN-13:9780692729526

DEDICATION

My loving husband, Melvin Porter

My daughters, O'She'Anna and Aquare'anna Porter

This dedication is to Everyone that knows me, my Family and Friends, Classmates, Church Family and to Everyone that allowed me to take just a little piece of your life and turned it into Poetry.

I dedicate this Book to you, Thank you

CONTENTS

Acknowledgments — vi

Introduction — 13

1. 100 Hillside Terrace — 17
2. My Eyes Were Opened — 19
3. I'm Too Close to the Mark — 23
4. My Ex-Lover — 25
5. I'm Suing the Church! — 31
6. A Countrified Love Story — 35
7. A Mother's Love — 45
8. A Prison Story — 47
9. A Woman's Worth is Priceless! — 51
10. A Wounded Heart — 53
11. Coldspring Battle Cry — 55

12	Candy Store – Man of My Dreams	57
13	*Finally Set Free*	59
14	For Such a Time as This…It takes Courage to Start and Faith to Finish	61
15	Good Bye	63
16	Wave over Wave	65
17	Family Reunion	67
18	I Wish There was Something More I could say	69
19	Legacy of Love	71
20	Love From a Friend's Heart	73
21	A Love Story	75
22	My First Love Left Me Today	79
23	Flashback in Time….	81

ACKNOWLEDGMENTS

I would first like to Thank the Lord my God for Blessing me with the Gifts and Talents that I have. I would also like to Thank my Pastors Jeff and Eileen Hackleman for constantly Encouraging me and Pouring the Word of God into my Spirit.

I would like to give a Special Thanks to my Wonderful Husband of fourteen years for his financial support. I would also like to Thank my Beautiful daughters for Believing in me when I wanted to give up and Encouraging me whole heartedly to Listen to God and following the Blueprint He has for me and my life.

I would like to Thank my Parents for having me because if there was No me you wouldn't have this Special Book in your Hands right now. I would Love to give a Super Special Thanks to my father: Carlton Teal, he is and was such a Major part of Encouraging me to be my Best and not Give Up even when times got hard. He was always there for me no matter the time or place. His Love is and was Always Unconditional towards me.

I Can't leave my Grandmother Dorothy J. Harrison out, it's because of her I am really detailed and vivid. I love you Grandma and Thank you. I would also like to give a Special Thanks to one of my Church Family members Mrs. Marsha Ceneskie-Parrott. If it had not been for her Persistently asking me to go to an Aglow International Meeting with her this Book would be a mere Dream. That leads me to my Final Thank you to Mrs. Edie Bayer, Thank you for working so hard on my Book and being so Patient with me. I Love each of you and Thank you so much for being in my life.

A Love Letter to the Author

To my beautiful wife whom I love so much, you are such a great blessing to our family. I have watched your struggle and I have lived through your pain. I am so very Proud of you for accomplishing what God has put in you. I am so Honored to be your right hand man, your Prayer Partner, your Best Friend, your Lover, your Biggest Supporter.

I enjoy listening to your ideas, stories, poems, poetry and work first hand, Hot off the Press as I call it. You are blessed with such an Awesome Gift and Beautiful talent. I truly know just how passionate you are about your writing and it just makes me love you more. I love to watch your face light up when you say I think I have a Masterpiece here.

I just wanted you to know that I Love you with all my Heart and I want you to keep on writing and listening to God. Remember to always follow your Heart. The Heart Never Lies, Congratulations Honey, and I look forward to reading a lot more of your work in the near Future.

        Your Loving Husband, Melvin A Porter

Letter to the Author: My Mom

Mom you are the best and you are always telling us that we can do all things through Christ Jesus who strengthens us. (Phil. 4:13) Well, through Christ you did it mom! You wrote your first book and we are so very proud of you. We can see the Excitement on your face, we are watching your Dreams come true. It warms our Heart to know that our mom the Author is doing what she loves doing the most, writing for the pure Enjoyment of others. This is just the beginning you can't Stop now you have more books inside of you. You must keep moving forward in God's Amazing Grace. We Love you Mom and Congratulations!

Love your daughters, O'She'Anna and Aquare'Anna

Words of Encouragement

Farrah Lecole Dee	Always be YOURSELF
Bonnie F. Reese	God's behind you all the way
Aquare'Anna P.	Keep on moving forward
O'She'Anna P.	Always be a light in a Dark place

Deborah Woodall	Fly and keep flying until you reach your Destination
Kelli Garrett Barlow	Truth and wisdom bring about a Holy Spirit restructuring transformation
Barbara Justice	Live on Purpose, walk by Faith and Laugh often

Benita Teal	Congratulations to my One and Only Extremely Talented Big Sister! I love you more than words can ever express. When Trials arise always press your way. Never be Discouraged, but Kneel down and Pray with Wisdom of his word and Knowledge.
Antonio Teal	This is just the Beginning to what you will accomplish Congratulations on your number on seller! I'm so Proud of your Big Sis. Love your Little Brother Tony!
Dawn Rushing	Continue to be bold, unmovable and unshakeable for Christ
Mellesha Porter	Be you ALWAYS no matter what keep your light and Smile everywhere you Go!
Betty Wheaton	God is your Shield, Fortress, Rock and Shepherd. He is for you so who can be against you.

To my forever friend and author of this book.

As my best friend your words have made me cry, made me laugh, given me knowledge and set me straight. I hope that the world will forever enjoy your words as much as I have over these last 30 years. I know that this is only the beginning cause you have so much to share. You have been a blessing to my life just as you have been to so many others. Great blessings to you in all of your future endeavors.

                Love always,

                Estella Jackson

INTRODUCTION

Hi, my name is Cloresa Porter and I am the first Author in my family to Publish her work. It's been a Battle but God is so Good to me. I started writing in fifth grade. It helped me to clear my mind and escape from the physical, mental, emotional and sexual abuse I grew up with.

I always knew I was Different and set Apart. I never really just fit in. I was always a Stand out kind of girl. I was just Blessed with the Gift of Laughter, Hope, Faith, Compassion, Thoughtfulness, Craziness, and on some rare occasions Stone Crazy.

Writing for me is a passion, I was Blessed with the Gift of words and knowing how to express them in Beautiful Masterpieces. This is why the Book you are about to read is so Important to me because my writing style is very different. I Truly am Different by Design, when God made me He made One of a Kind. (Jer. 1:5)

I have been Happily married to my Sexy Chocolate God Fearing Supportive husband Melvin Porter for fourteen years now and I was Blessed with two Amazing Beautiful God Ordained daughters, O'She'Anna and Aquare'Anna Porter.

My life is so Amazing because of my Family and Friends. I Love Living Life on Purpose, I Love writing from my Heart and getting Instant Downloads from the Lord. I hope you Enjoy what you read to the fullest. Remember sharing is caring, you just might be in my next Masterpiece. God Bless each of you.

I Am Different by Design!

Cloresa Porter

Chapter 1

☹ 100 Hillside Terrace (The Story) ☹

100 Hillside Terrace is its own little community that keeps our own local San Jacinto county police up on their feet. They enter these apartments not once but twice a week. Who am I kidding, it may even be more, I know there's someone else out there besides me who is keeping the score.

100 Hillside Terrace is so sad, you see, there is always mess surrounding me. Whether it be next door or right down the way, there is always somebody around here that has something damaging to say.

Don't get me wrong these apartments have done no wrong. It's the people that just can't seem to get along. He said, she said, squash that mess and leave it dead.

Grown people cursing, fussing, and fighting all the time. What kind of examples are we setting for our young children to see, beside mommy or daddy just wanting to be seen, walking around here acting all tough and mean.

100 Hillside Terrace has too much jealousy, and to top that off a lot of negativity. There's drugs and violence, sitting around chilling, gossiping and stealing, late night dealing, those cradle robbing villains, heathenish heathens, trash talking demons and childish grown people.

And let's not forget those child molesters that prey on the low, the humble, and meek. I know you probably didn't want to hear my story or it might have made you sick, but I take my words that I wrote and I plead the fifth. That would be freedom of speech, especially when it's true.

So let me start off by saying I want to apologize to you if this 100 Hillside Terrace story offends you. I guess that means it hit close to home and that you need to stop doing all your evil, dirt and wrong. But if you like this story and you too feel that it is true, just know that you're not alone and you do have someone that agrees with you.

Chapter 2

My Eyes Were Opened

Today is a day like no other. It all started with my alarm, my alarm not going off on time and me over sleeping. So as my curtains opened up and the sun came in the glow of the rays shined upon my face.

As I looked around I realized that I was staring into another face. "My God what just happened here? Why are you in my bed?"

Then he looked at me with a slight smile and said, "You don't remember? You let me in."

"What does this mean?" as I caught my breath.

He said, "Your love is poison and nothing less!"

"How did we end up at this point and you in my bed?"

He said, "Your secret life has caught up with you!"

As I felt this feeling of numbness cover my body from head to toe, I said, "You get out and don't come back no more!"

He said, "Well stop inviting me in with this revolving door."

"What do you mean?" I was in total shock.

He said, "If you play with fire you will get burned. It's just hard for some people to learn."

"Please stop talking in parables and just tell me the truth!"

He said, "I am what I am to the things that you do. Like sleeping with a different man night after night, and doing things with your body that you know ain't right. I can't forget, porn and the list just goes on and on."

By this time my mouth was on the floor, and can't stop my heart from racing anymore. "I want you to leave just get out of my house and don't you ever come here again."

He said, "Just let me gather my things. I will be going but I will be back because you repeat this same routine night after night."

Tears just streamed down my face and I felt so misplaced for what he was saying was all so true. Now I'm just lost and I don't know just what to do.

Then just like that the phone started to ring and a voice on the other line was just saying all sorts of things.

"What, who is this? I know you are joking right? Wait, don't go! Someone says they have a video of us last night!" We were both in shock and had this look on our face. "Where can I meet you?" and "When will this be?

I caught a chill because the voice on the other end sounded so familiar to me. So I dressed myself and we ran out the door, only to end up face down on the floor. It was a trap and we both had been played.

The cameras were still rolling as we wiped tears from our eyes, and with one glance we spotted a sign that said, 'You are not alone! We are watching you, and the moment you think that we can't see is the moment we plug in and the whole world sees!'

Whoa! What had we gotten ourselves into?

"Who are you and where did you come from?"

"Just go along with whatever they say or we could be in for trouble today."

Needless to say my whole life flashed before my eyes!

And then I saw all the soul ties. I needed help for what I was seeing was much too strong. All this time I thought it was a man and it was a Sex Demon holding my hand.

Wow, I bet you didn't see that coming and neither did I!

Not all that he was saying was a total lie. I realized that I had opened gateways with all my sin and just kept inviting the demons in. One by one and some brought friends to torment me again and again.

Then in the Blink of an eye I heard my alarm clock go off and I felt this amazing feeling inside.

I popped out of bed and grabbed my Head and realized that I had been sleeping with and talking with a Sex Demon. He was a very *'familiar spirit'* to me.

My God! I started thanking God for another chance and showing me where I went wrong. I quickly repented for my sin and never again used my body to do so much harm as opening up gateways and make the demons so strong.

THE MORAL OF THE STORY IS: SOUL TIES ARE REAL AND DEMONS ARE TOO. SEX DEMONS REALLY DO EXIST, AND WHEN YOU DON'T REPENT AND TURN FROM YOUR WICKED, EVIL WAYS ALL YOU ARE DOING IS FEEDING THEM WITH SIN AND ALLOWING THEM TO BECOME STRONGER AND STRONGER IN YOUR LIFE.

Chapter 3

I'm too Close to the Mark

"On your mark! Get ready! Set! Go!"

Those are the words I heard as I tied my shoe at the starting line.

Wait, I'm not ready to go, wait, that's so not fair. But I refuse to give up or give in I've come too far to quit now.

So I will press toward the mark of the 'High Calling'.

Yes! Finally I am passing everyone that left me behind. You can just get lost because you are going down. I am the winner, I am the leader, I am, I am, and I am in the lead in this race now. I'm too close to the Mark to fall behind.

I must steady my body and steady my mind. I need You

Lord to show up now and help me on with an extra push.

Then I heard a small voice say, "Child, My child! When will you learn that fast is not always better and you just might get burned? I know that you are close to the mark and that is so very good but I want you to stop and think about the humble spirit that got you there and the prideful spirit that can take you away. You are starting to use the "I-word" a lot, and that is so self-centered. That's taking me out and begging for me to come again."

My face went blank and my spirit started to cry.

I stopped right there, dead in my tracks as others passed me by. I fell to my knees. "Lord, please forgive me of this awful sin! This is not how I want to win!"

THE MORAL OF THE STORY IS:

SLOW AND STEADY WILL WIN THE RACE AND FAST AND SELF RIGHTEOUS WILL LEAVE YOU IN LAST PLACE.

Chapter 4

MY EX- LOVER

Come! Go with me as I take you for a roller coaster ride inside my mind.

It was a Saturday night around 7:45 P.M. and I was watching my favorite T.V. show, *When Lust turns Deadly*.

I started having a flashback of when we met, and as I sat there I didn't know what to expect. When all of a sudden the phone rang out of the blue and on the other end was my Ex-Lover saying, "Girl, I want you!"

My heart fell and I got this feeling that caused me to scream and say, "You know where I live it hasn't changed!"

Wait! What did I just say? "Stop! I can't, I mean, we can't!"

He said, "We can't what?"

"You know, you are my Ex-Lover for a reason."

"Well", he said, "Okay I'll get there in an hour or two and when I show up you know just what to do."

As I hang up the phone my heart is racing and I have this excitement of anticipation that is pouring over my body and I can't stop thinking about what he said. I am now shivering and my knees are weak my speech is slurred and I can hardly speak.

"God, Oh, God help me right now. This is so sinful, I know, but I already told him No, No, No."

So as I walked into my bathroom to try and calm down, I heard a knock at my door. Sweet Jesus my heart just hit the floor! I just stood there frozen in fear, and I heard my husband say, "What is it, Dear?"

"Are you expecting company this time of night?"

I'm trying to think but I just have this blank look upon my face.

"Honey, are you ok?"

"No, it's my Ex-Lover and he came to play."

"Wait! What did you just say?"

"I said it's my Ex-Lover and he came to play."

"Okay, let me get up and I will handle this. Is this dude crazy? Do he really want my fist?"

Well, right about the time my husband got out of bed I almost fainted, so I grabbed my head. "Lord this is so not funny! Please tell me why?"

Then I heard the Lord say, "You will learn tonight."

"Lord, please teach me another way!"

Then he said, "Daughter, kneel and pray."

My husband answered the door and then I heard my Ex-Lover say, "Where your wife at?"

My husband said, "Naw, man, it's not going down like that tonight."

My husband said, "Come on in and sit right down because I have a message for you that will turn that smile upside down."

Then my husband called my name and said, "Sit right down alongside of your Ex-Lover because this is for the both of you. I have known now for quite some time that you two have been playing around.

"But you see the Jesus that lives in me wants you to know that you are forgiven because you can't hurt me. You have to repent and get right with God. Adultery is far from God's Heart."

Okay, I think I just peed my pants, because did he just say that he already knew and that we are forgiven, too? Lord, my Lord I repent of my sins and I promise I will never go through this mess again.

I sure wish you could've seen the look on my Ex-Lover's face when my loving husband gave him a warm embrace. The tears streamed down his face as he asked my husband to please forgive him for all of his wrong. He told my husband I said, "No", but he wanted me anyway so he came.

My husband said, "I know. God told me. Now was the time for this to end, because ya'll were getting too comfortable in your sin."

My husband told my Ex-Lover, "Now it's time for you to go, and don't you ever come to my house anymore. What you had is over and done. God Bless you and have a Good night."

Then he looked at me and said, "Well, Hon, it's time for bed. I have to get up early for work in the morning. I love you and good night."

I went to sleep thanking the Lord and saying, "I am forgiven, I am forgiven."

THE MORAL OF THE STORY IS:

TO BE FORGIVEN YOU MUST FORGIVE, NO MATTER HOW HARD OR UNREALISTIC YOU THINK IT MIGHT BE.

Chapter 5

I'M SUING THE CHURCH

Hi! My name is Joy Faith Love McPorter. This is my story because I am suing my church -- The Beacon of Light Holy Temple Inner Faith 2nd Baptist Evangelistic One Way Christian Center on Mount Calvary Angelic Way.

I hurt myself last Sunday because I chose to move before the Spirit did, and started running and jumping and falling all out. There was no one there to catch me when I fell, and I felt my back immediately swell.

Later on when the worship team was singing a song I misjudged a note and sang it all wrong. Now my throat is sore and no one really cares so I'm suing my church because they just aren't fair.

Now came time for the preacher to preach and he spoke so hard he spit on my cheek. That's just nasty and I could die from that so I told him after church and he laughed with not a worry or care. What about my cheek Pastor, what about me?

Well, it's time for 2:00 o'clock service and I overheard the deacon say, "Don't let Sister Joy come past the second row of chairs. You know how she gets around ramps and stairs." Well, that's discrimination and that sure isn't fair! So I just took that to my Lord in Prayer.

Around 2:35 P.M. was altar call so when I started to the altar I was stopped at row two and the Prayer Warrior Hit me with a one-two, one-two. Smack in the center of my head and said, "Loose her!" I hit the floor with no one there again, but this time when I came up I was really mean.

I said, "Now this foolishness must stop!" and all the deacons said, "No! You have to Stop!" with an angry kind of shout.

I was so confused and didn't know what to say, so I fell out again and this time I just stayed. They left me right there with my skirt over my head and threw a cover over me like I was just dead. I felt so embarrassed and so ashamed, so I just started to call the Preacher names!

He said, "Get up from there and go back to your seat! Because you are being a distraction to the saints of God, one more outburst and I will pull your member card!"

Now that comment just broke my heart, so I'm going to sue my church. I talked with my Lawyer just yesterday and she told me I was lucky they didn't throw me out and rebuke all the hell right out of me!

What I gave 300 dollars for that? "So, I take it, you aren't going to help me sue my church?"

"Nope, because you weren't doing any of God's Work!"

THE MORAL OF THE STORY IS:

STOP PLAYING CHURCH AND GET A REAL RELATIONSHIP WITH GOD. SUING THE CHURCH WON'T BRING YOU CLOSER TO GOD BUT ONLY EXPOSES YOUR EVIL INTENT TO DO WRONG AND WANT OTHERS TO UPHOLD YOU IN YOUR MESS AND WRONG DOINGS.

Chapter 6

A Countrified Love Story

Let me take you back in time, when falling in love should've been a crime. The season is summer going into fall. I have a love for puppies that's plain to see. I got one from my mother's friend and she went everywhere with me. I named her 'Brown Sugar'. She was fluffy and fat, light brown and she loved to snack.

At this time I was living in Beaumont, traveling back and forth between Oakhurst and Beaumont. Sometimes I would leave Sugar at home if I knew I wouldn't be gone long. She was my baby, my house puppy. She shopped at Pets Mart, she was up to date on all her shots and she ate what I ate. But my grandma and her children didn't like dogs, puppies, cats or any other animal and the shock of bringing one into her house was devastating and all so wrong.

But, I just couldn't leave her in the car alone, in the heat and sometimes cold. So I went to my cousin's house one day and she has two children and they love puppies. So I told her I would give Brown Sugar to her and when I go home on the weekend then I would bring back her food, and shampoo, shot records and all her stuff. She said, "Ok."

About three days later I went back and much to my surprise, she had given Brown Sugar away to her so-called best friend. I could not believe that she did that to me. Brown Sugar was my baby; my love for her was great!

So when my cousin saw the look of lost hope on my face she said, "Wait! My friend is a great person and she will care for your puppy and won't hurt her." I didn't feel much peace because I didn't know this person. My heart was broken and in my mind my baby was gone forever. I just wanted my Brown Sugar back.

So one day I was visiting my cousin and we were talking about life. Her phone starts to ring, she looked at the caller ID and says, "Oh! No! I don't want to talk to her! She is wearisome."

I said, "Who?"

She replied, "A friend."

Then I quickly replied, "The friend that has my puppy."

She said, "Yes."

I said, "I would like to answer the phone to find out how my puppy is doing. "

She said, "Go ahead."

I then answered the phone and said, "Hello! Are you the lady that has my baby?"

She said, "I don't have nobody's baby."

I said, "Brown Sugar, my puppy."

She laughed and said, "Yes. I do have your puppy and she is fine. Do you want to come and see her?"

I said, "Yes." But I didn't know where she lived, so she offered to come and get me.

When I hung up the phone, my cousin said, "What did she say?"

I said, "She said she was on her way to come and get me."

My cousin then said, "If she said it then she will do it."

Sure enough about an hour or two later she showed up in this beat up orange Chevrolet pickup truck. I got a little scared. But my cousin told me it was ok, and safe to go with her.

I was not thinking to take my own car and follow her so I rode with her and we went past Point Blank, past Onalaska, and into Blanchard, Texas. I grew up in the back woods of Oakhurst, Texas but never have I ever stepped foot into Blanchard.

It was close to dark and I was a little skeptical about the whole drive anyway. All she could talk about was how pretty I was and how her husband saw me at a church revival and was staring at me and she told him she would slap him if he looked at me again.

Wow! I was only focused on Jesus, not an adulterous sin.

Now she is bringing me to her house. Wow! Then she kept saying how her brother that is forty-three years old would really like me because I was twenty-four years old. She said that he had just come out of a really bad relationship and he was living with her until he got himself together and got back on his feet. I just kept looking at her saying, "No, thank you. I don't want your brother."

Although in my mind I knew I love older men, one day true love I will find. I just have an attraction for them. It's in my DNA. I was judging her because she was heavy set and I didn't find her attractive. So I figured her brother would be the same. I do not date heavy set or big, horrible looking men.

So all of a sudden the truck broke down at night in the middle of nowhere. She said her foot hit a wire. All I heard was water from Lake Livingston.

There was a phone booth with no phone in the booth, and no houses around us. Then to top it all off she told me to stay with the truck and wait while so went for help to call a taxi. I said, "There are no taxis in the country, in the back woods!" She said, "Yes, there is." and she walked away, leaving me to walk and pray, and paced around that old beat up truck praying and singing to God.

I prayed, "Lord, please don't let her kill me and my family not know where I am!"

Then about 30 minutes later, around the corner came a taxi and she popped out. I thanked the Lord with everything in me and was in so much shock! I got in and we went to her house, deeper into the woods.

When we pulled up to her trailer, this sexy, dark brown,

muscle bound, bald-headed man was standing on the steps of the trailer. He was wearing a white muscle shirt, and starched-down jeans with holes that stood to attention. My eyes had never before seen holes starched in denim jeans.

He was so sexy to me I tried asking her, "Was that your brother?"

She told me, "Yeah!" and to leave her alone, since she was talking to the taxi driver about business, and now go on.

So, I had to walk right past him to get to my puppy that she had outside and tied to a tree. I knew I had to speak but nothing more. Therefore, I quickly spoke and went past him very fast. He smiled and spoke back.

Then after I came from visiting Brown Sugar in the yard everybody went into the trailer. So I knocked on the door, and she said, "Come on in, sister-in-law!" She was already claiming me. She said her brother's name was Melvin. I said, "Hi, Melvin!" He was standing in the kitchen with a pan of baked chicken in his hands. He had just cooked dinner.

They invited me to eat with them. I was very hungry, but I couldn't show it. So, I said, "No, thank you. I am not hungry. Besides, you might try to poison me, and take my precious goods."

He laughed and said, "I wouldn't do that."

So after about three tries I said, "I guess I can eat, knowing my backbone was touching my feet."

So we ate and watched TV for a while. Then when I was ready to go his sister said, "You know I have to go to the Woodlands tomorrow to pick up my son. I can take you back then."

Wow! There went another shocker. Only my cousin knew who I left with, and not exactly where I was. So I was allowed to call her for a short time, because it was long distance from her house to my cousin's house.

I told my cousin that her friend said she would bring me back tomorrow when she came from the Woodlands. My cousin told me to watch myself because she was a little crazy.

I said, "Wow! Now you tell me! You first told me I was safe. I did not think to bring my own car or a can of mace! And if I would have chosen to stay on my own then I would have had my overnight bag that I keep in the trunk for emergencies."

His sister said, "We look about the same size."

I said, "Oh, no we are not!"

She said, "I might have something that can fit you." So she went and looked and me and Melvin watched movies and laughed. She came out of the room with this beautiful red and black teddy. Melvin smiled from ear to ear.

He said, "Yeah! She can wear that."

I said, "No. What about a night gown or big shirt?"

She gave me a robe to cover myself. I went to bathe and came out fresh and clean and smelling really nice. I then sat on the sofa beside Melvin. He kept wanting to touch me, and I kept moving his hand. His sister went to her room so we could talk.

I told him I would sleep on the couch and he could have his room. I wanted to be near the front door. Then, he said he would sleep on the couch and I could sleep in his room.

I said, "Ok, but am I doomed?"

So when I got ready to go into his room, he said, "Wait! How about you sleep in my bed and I sleep on the floor next to the bed?"

I said, "Oh! Like a guard dog! Ok."

So he went into the room and I went to the bath room before bed. When I came out I went into the room and just burst out laughing. He started laughing so hard. I said, "You got me good!" His bed was only a mattress and his mattress was already on the floor! I said, "That was a good one!" So we laid down together and laughed and talked for hours before we fell asleep in each other's arms.

There was a sweet peace in the midst of my inner storm. The next morning his sister said, "You must not have done anything with my brother because I didn't hear any noises.

I thought, "What a sick person to try to listen to her brother make out with another woman!"

I told him and he said, "She didn't say that, did she?"

So, after that night we made a major connection and throughout the summer we spent time together and went out to different places and evening fishing dates. After his sister saw that our relationship was serious then she started to change and say, "Brother! You don't need to be with that young thang!"

But, we would let nothing and no one stop our love for each other. About three months later we were married and had a baby on the way. His sister also tried to tell him that our baby was not his child. He didn't fall for it.

We have faced lots of long, hard trials and tribulations from both sides of our family, but not one of us has ever given up and called it quits. We know have a home, four vehicles and two businesses that we run. We have two beautiful children together and seven total. We do have the American dream and a countrified love story to match.

THE MORAL OF THE STORY IS:

WHAT WAS MEANT FOR BAD, HURT, PAIN, EVIL, NEGATIVE, DEVALUING, SHAMEFULNESS OR SELF RIGHTEOUSNESS WAS TURNED INTO A BEAUTIFUL COUNTRYFIED LOVE STORY.

SO FOLLOW YOUR HEART AND PRAY ABOUT YOUR FEARS AND MAYBE, JUST MAYBE GOING WITH STRANGERS WON'T GET YOU KILLED. REMEMBER WHAT GOD HAS FOR YOU IS FOR YOU AND SOMETIMES HE USES ANIMALS TO GUIDE YOU INTO DESTINY.

Chapter 7

A Mother's Love

A mother's love is never hurtful, it will never do you any harm, nor will it allow you to weep, cry, or moan.

A mother's love, will never down you, or curse you, but it will convict your wrong. A mother's love is most gentle and it shelters you from the storm.

A mother's love is all so sweet, there is not another that can compete. A mother's love has no envy towards her child. When she sees you it's always a pleasant smile.

A mother's love does not divide. She doesn't see you any lesser than another child or two. A mother's love is sent from above, to cover you up like a warm, summer, heartfelt hug.

A mother's love never talks bad about her young. She encourages her child to be their best, and if they ever come in last place, then it's just a test. To go again and give it your all and try not to stumble and you will not fall.

A mother's love is so complete! It's love, it's music. To repeat, it's a sound of harmony and sweet whispers by the powers that be. A mother's love, that's what's in me. And I will pass it on to my little babies... you just wait and see.

A Mother's Love

Chapter 8

A PRISON STORY

Have you ever felt pain, from head to toe, screamed to the top of your voice so much, that you couldn't talk no more? Have you ever been right but accused of being wrong? Have you prayed all day and all night long? Have you tried to cope with the thought of never seeing your family again? All because some liar called you his so-called friend.

Well this is my story. This is my chance to tell the world that I am sick of being left behind, sick of doing another man's time. For what? A silly crime. I did not beat and kill that little old maid, I was only trying to get paid.

I left her room at a quarter till noon, told her, "Sorry, Miss but we are through." Then passing me up was a male dressed in red, holding a letter saying, "Man, she's dead."

"Just wait until Iget my hands on her. I will choke her to no end, then repeat if I have to do it again!"

I left there as fast as I could, thinking I just got lucky that will not be good. But, before I could make it through the first door, the police were already standing at my car.

They said, "Is your name Wade?"

I said, "Please don't lean against my car."

"You are wanted for a murder that took place in room 303c. A little old hand maid is dead."

I said, "Don't look at me, I only got paid and then I was on my way. But I did see a man about 6'2" with a blue shirt and green shorts and flip flops speed pass me holding a letter in his hand, saying he would kill her when he got his hands on her."

"Please come with us," as they read my rights. They didn't want to hear a word. Their minds were already made up. I put up a fight because this sounds like a set up to me. Who would want to get rid of me?

After the struggle and after the fight, I felt a quick

punch upside my head. Then I felt a swift kick up my back side and I screamed for help. I just lowered my head because the cops just keep saying the little old maid was dead.

How do I prove that it's not true? A court appointed lawyer that did me no good. I was sent to prison on my first trial, I looked over at the jury and they all smiled.

They sent me to a prison far away from home, men attacking me all night long. When I fight one, two more would come. Then I started praying, "Devil, leave me alone. Jesus I need you now more than ever. I will always serve you forever and ever. Please send down your angels to protect me each day, this is my prison story and I will try not to cry. Just know that I will confess to be innocent until I die. But, the question that keeps coming to my mind is who would do this to me and why? (Prison Story)

THE MORAL OF THE STORY IS:

KNOW WHO IS IN YOUR CIRCLE AND WEED OUT THE KILLER WEEDS. NOT EVERYONE IS YOUR FRIEND AND NOT EVERY FRIEND IS A TRUE FRIEND OR THE FRIEND YOU NEED.

Chapter 9

A Woman's Worth is Priceless!

She can deal with stress and carry heavy burdens.

She smiles when she feels like screaming and sings when she feels like crying.

She cries when she's happy and laughs when she's afraid.

Her love is unconditional, her wisdom is graced with age.

There's only one thing wrong with her, she forgets what she is worth! She lowers her value and will settle for less.

So next time you look in the mirror, take a good long

look. You are beautiful inside and out. Take time to focus on yourself and just sit back and relax for the day.

You have value and you have worth! You are God's masterpiece that was formed out of the dirt. You have hidden treasures not yet seen. They are buried deep within.

God handpicked you to be the best you that you can be.

> You are worth more than rubies and priced higher than gold.

> You are a set of rare pearls and can't be bought, found, caught, stolen or sold.

> Your eyes shine like diamonds hidden in the rough.

> And when you speak it's like platinum floating by.

> Your value is more than you will ever know so take a deep breath and let your beauty show.

Soft, sweet words of a humming bird is what your spirit sends when you signal the winds and praise his Name for victory you do proclaim. A woman's worth is more precious than you'll ever know. It's a glimpse into heaven and an eternity of love.

Chapter 10

A Wounded Heart

Please go with me back in time as I uncover the story of a wounded heart. I have a wounded heart that needs to be fixed. I have been hurt in so many ways my pain has lasted for days and days. When will this hurt go away? To top it all off it feels good in a way.

I will try to break it down for you to understand. You know it all started with a man. This guy was my so-called friend. I did for him what I've done for no man. He said he wanted me and my son, he said he loved us ... just as long as he could be right and do no wrong.

I went through hell and back with him. My mother hated the cold hard truth. For six years this hurt and pain went on, 'til I woke up and said I'm gone. Never, not once did I cheat on him, but he cheated on me and left my emotions out on a limb.

I left this man, my so called friend, found my own place, but could still see his face. He would come over every now and then, and we would still sleep together what a sin. Now, time has passed and I've made an ass. I'm sick to my stomach and feeling so bad, could this be the signs of a seed gone bad.

What will I do when he say I'm a lie? All I can do is cry, cry, cry. I have no one I'm all alone. My stupidity has left me deafly tone. Who do I turn to, what do I do?

Let's be honest, it's time for the truth. I can't do this all on my own, I need some help from someone strong. I need the Lord! Please hear my cry, and Lord please don't pass me by! I'm at my lowest point you see, and I know now you can help me.

Please forgive me of my sins and set my soul free. I'm sick of living in this type of misery.

Chapter 11

COLDSPRING BATTLE CRY

It's the name of Jesus & The Glory of our God, anybody, everybody put that in your hearts. There's a day a'coming where the thundering will be roaring, the lighting will be flashing and the trumpets will be blowing and the sound of our Lord will quickly be a'coming.

And on our honor we will proudly stand giving our pledge to God with our right hand. We'll be fasting & praying and standing firm throughout the land. Giving praises to our God because, yes, we can, amazed at His Glory as it covers all the land.

It's the name of Jesus and the glory of our God, anybody, everybody put that in your hearts. We give

God praises with all of our heart, pouring out all our soul, so He can give us more. In the Name of Jesus and the Glory of our God this is our "Battle Cry" that sets us apart.

DEDICATED TO FAMILY FAITH, COLDSPRING

Chapter 12

**CANDY STORE
MAN OF MY DREAMS**

I Feel like a kid in the Candy Store, Every time I see you I just want more.

Your loving (boy) makes me so insane, it's like Dove Milk Chocolate all over my Brain.

I love, I love to see you sweat, it's like Lemon Drops, I get so soaking wet.

Your love, your love, just takes me away. It's like a Calgon bath on a Cold Winter's Day.

My Heart, my Heart is so Renewed it feels like the First time I met Jesus, when I saw you.

Oh, how Oh, could this be, your Love is so Sweet it just Hurts my teeth.

Your Soft and Gentle Warm and Loving Hands Caress my Body and lead me to Understand

Why I Chose you to be my Man. Every time I look at you I can't help but see my Heart's Desires running so Wild and Free. I just want a piece of Chocolate 'cause you're so Good to me.

Chapter 13

Finally Set Free

Release the fat from under my skin.

Release the fat stored within.

Favor, Lord, in Jesus Name, take away these hunger pains. I will not feed an Idol god, for if I do destruction won't be far.

I take back the Life that God has given me and insert it with Victory. Mercy and Grace shall cover me. No more Idols that just make fun of me.

I was trying to fill a void that couldn't be filled. Because God can't be Replaced with Food. I just allowed the enemy to make a Fool out of me and Rub it in my Face.

Release the fat from under my skin. Release the fat that's stored within. Sin is Sin No matter what kind, you will be set Free when you get this through your mind.

No more settling for less than the Best. I will give the devil a run for his money and past my Test. You don't Control me anymore, I Control you now hit the door.

You don't tell me when to eat, I'll let you know when I want a piece of meat. Stop your whining and complaining so, because reality just checked in and you win no more.

Feed me, Feed me is what you say, but my Ears No longer want Entertain & Play. You have taken up far too much of my space, stopping me from Living because Food has taken that Place.

I Serve an Awesome and Powerful God one that can Truly look in and See my Heart. All that Fat is Hindering me from being the woman that God has called me to be.

So on this Day I make a Stand, loose her Satan, Release my Hand. I Declare and I Decree that God will Live and Reign in me. I take back my Power and my Authority, I take back my Life that God has given me.

Release this Hurt and Release this Pain, Release all this Stored up Fat in Jesus Name...

My Body is a Temple for the Most High God, and I must Protect it at all Cost. Don't let Satan make a Fool out of you with putting things in your Body you are not Supposed to.

Chapter 14

For Such a Time as This....
It takes Courage to Start and Faith to Finish.

I made it, through all my ups and downs, through all my heartaches and frowns. Through all my disappointments, heartbreaks and turn downs.

I made it, though each week meant learning new Stuff. I Promised myself I would not give up. I held on to Gods Unchanging Hand, and Prayed and Fasted so that I could Understand. Lord Lead and Guide me, is this the Right way. Then I heard his Gentle voice say " My child, My child please Stop doubting me, School of Ministry is the Place to Be. Many will Start but few will Finish. When you Obey my Word you Strengthen your Family's Reborn Lineage.

I made it, for 9 whole months, through the Storm. The Rain, The Hell, The Sleet and The Snow, and even when I had little energy The Lord said "My child get up and Go".

I made it for such a Time as This, to Minister to God's People, and Heal the Sick. To Witness to all not just a Quick Fix.

It took all the Courage I had to Step out on Faith and be a Proud Grad. Even though I made a few Mistakes. This means New Levels of Love, and Wisdom are coming my way.

New Levels of Respect, because God is making a Way. New Levels of Forgiveness, and Unity in my personal Sphere. A New Understanding that I can Understand, no longer does the Lord have to Hold my Hand.

I am ready for the field, experience a must, or I can just let go and have Faith, Believe, Obey and Trust, always be a Willing Vessel and God will do the Rest. He loves to watch me while I'm taking my Test.

For Such a Time as This, I just walked across that stage with a YOU go Saint LOOK upon my FACE, and a I made it, Grace as I took my Place. Roll Call are you here, the School of Ministry can stand and Cheer for we made it through another year..

It took Courage to Start and Faith to Finish, and I made it, Praise I (we) did it.....   School of Ministry

Chapter 15

GOOD BYE

You never, ever wanted me. Now I'm foot loose and fancy free.

Can you please stop calling my phone?

I just want to be left alone.

You said that you love me and I'm the only one

but that was determined a lie

when I looked through your phone

and it made me cry.

You never, ever wanted me. Now I'm foot loose and fancy free.

Moving on so I say so long

to my past and I welcome my future with open arms.

GOODBYE

Chapter 16

WAVE OVER WAVE

Wave over wave came crashing over me as I felt a rush of satisfaction flood my mind, soul and body. I am now stuck between space and time riding a wave of endless love.

This feeling I am feeling is higher than ecstasy. I'm floating and I feel so transparent, you can see straight through me.

I feel so free and I feel no attachments to this world.

No soul ties and free from sin. It's a feeling that the world just can't explain when you allow Jesus to come in. Wave over wave came crashing over me as I felt a rush of Satisfaction blow straight through me.

Wave over Wave gives me an amazing rush, and I got that off of just one touch. A touch that no man can give, now don't that just give you chills.

Baptize me in your Spirit and wash me with your blood.

Wave over wave of your amazing unending love.

Chapter 17

Happy One Year Anniversary

To my Big Bro'...

Dennis Wyatt

Happy one year anniversary January 16, 2015 to a brother whom I love. Just thinking back to a year ago when I stepped out on faith and knocked on your door. I heard, "Come in," and saw you sitting there. My heart beat got faster as I yielded to the Master.

Just when you thought it would be another ordinary day, God showed up in an amazing way. God knows your heart and just what you need. He knew you wanted to know if your father had produced any other seeds. Lol...

Well, he answered you on January 16, 2014 and up popped a sister you had never seen. Then in even more amazement you asked about your Dad and his placement. Just the shocker you needed I knew just where he was, and there went the Hugs!

Uniting and Reuniting is a feeling out this world. Just like trusting God when he pours out His love. I Love you Big Bro'.

        Happy One Year Anniversary

            (Family Reunion)

Chapter 18

I wish there was something more I could say

I wish there was something I could say to ease your pain, but peace comes with the smell of glorious morning rain. Sweet memories of yesterday's past will sustain you till you meet again. He will be there to welcome you with a celebration of family and friends, standing at the 'Pearly Gates' with a smile upon his face.

Family and friends will surround you with love and support. God will comfort you with strength and hope. I wish there was something I could say to ease your pain, but peace comes with the smell of glorious morning rain.

It's okay to mourn, it's okay to cry, just know that Jesus is right there holding you in the middle of the night. Matthew 5:4 says, "Blessed are they that mourn, for they shall be comforted."

God gave you a mighty warrior, a loyal husband, a lover, a friend. God gave you His best and nothing less. God gave you just what you needed to make it this far. nNow the Holy Spirit will lead, guide and direct your heart.

We Love you so and will do whatever you need; so, we will leave you some scriptures upon which to stand firm.

(Ps. 18:2, Ps. 18:28, Ps. 73:26, Ps. 23, Ps. 34:18, Ps. 61:2, John 14:1-3, Matt. 11:28, 2 Cor. 12:9)

Chapter 19

Legacy of Love

A song of love that makes me sing.
A love that makes the whole world
Sing. To me you bring a million flowers
In one dream. It's like a picture with
A frame you're just so valuable like
A window of love for all to see

Love

Anna

Cloresa Porter

Chapter 20

Love from a Friend's Heart

I thought about you today, and wondered how you are. I was a little upset at the fact that you were out sick last week and didn't open your mouth to speak. How dare you be in the hospital and not say a word? What if I wanted to travel to see my new home girl? The thought of you laying there with no family or friends around just made me upset again, and made these words spin around.

I know you are a big girl and can take care of yourself, but what happens when you fight, fight, fight and you have no fight left? You need the prayers of the righteous to availeth much, and to see many smiling faces to keep you deeply in touch. I know this may sound like fussing, but I missed you so. Knowing you weren't on a business trip but healing in many ways, just brought me back to reality that it pays to stay prayed.

Next time, whenever you are in need, please open your mouth with great speed so I can start to pray and intercede. I can understand not telling everyone, but the ones you love and trust I see it as a must.

I thought about you today, and wondered if you are okay. Then I took a moment of silence to pray. "Lord, please bless and heal Ms.Cat today. Send her angels to pave her way, and cover her with your precious blood and protect her in every way. Amen"

DEDICATED TO MS. CATHERINE LERMA - MY FRIEND

Chapter 21

A Love Story

The night was long and his stay was short. I tried not to give in, but that would be too smart. I love this man so, but his wife will not let him go.

His face was the finest I'd ever seen. His touch was innocent, sweet and clean. His whisper in my ear was all so soft. The sound of his voice let me know he was the boss. This tall, dark and muscle bound man holds me every chance he can.

I love this man day or night, but he can only love me when the time is right. How could this be, how did I stoop so low? Why can't I let this married man go?

I'm afraid of being all alone. What if something goes terribly wrong? Then again, and again I will sing this same sad love song. The night was long and his stay was short, just looking at him I'm having naughty thoughts.

All these thoughts of me and him ... I am putting my emotions out on a limb. Just to be his boo, his girl, his fling. That just gives me joy enough to sing!

But, I'm tired of being in the dark, living a lie that's tearing me apart. I must confront his wife when I can. I have to do this! I must make a stand. But, how do I break to my sister I want her husband? I know this may sound sick, or out of your league, but leave it to me to bring a family to its knees.

What will she say, or what will she do, knowing that we are blood -- will she be through? Or will she understand and say, "He's all on you!" Will she try to hurt me in any way? If so, I hope it's not today. I know, this love affair is wrong, and it's been going on for far too long.

The night was long and his stay was short. I promised him, I crossed my heart, that I would not tell his beautiful wife. Now, that's a crazy sacrifice, knowing it could end my life, and leave him cheating on his wife.

The day is hot and my mind is made up, I called my sister

and said, "Let's have lunch -- today at noon at the Cheaters Saloon." I told her to meet me at table three.

She said, "Girl, you would never believe that Justin has been cheating on me!"

I looked at her in such disbelief, and thought to myself, "My! What a relief! She knows he is cheating on her but, with who? Her baby sister, Mary Lou."

I looked her dead in her eyes, and said, "Surprise, Sarah. He's cheating on you with me, and I am 15 weeks pregnant with his child -- a mom to be. You're going to be his Aunty and Stepmother! Isn't that wild."

She had no joking in her blood. She glanced at me and turned straight thug! She whipped out a gun and said, "Nigga', what? How could you do this to me? Blood is thicker than water, at least I thought, Mary.

"Mary Lou, just get out my face, for to look at you now is a real disgrace. I came here today to tell you that Justin was not only cheating on me, but that he also had AIDS -- and who ever this person is don't have very many days.

"For Justin is sick and his health is fading fast, and that our love will soon be a part of the past. But, now to look at you and see his AIDS has traveled through my family. I guess you wonder why I never told you. It's because I never thought in a million years that you would stoop so low!

"You knew me and Justin weren't having sex, so this was your big chance to show Justin you could fulfill his desires, his dreams and more. Now, you are stuck with two packages you can never get rid of - all in the name of lust, greed, sin, and so-called love!"

THE MORAL OF THIS STORY IS:

IF HE DON'T BELONG TO YOU KEEP HIM OUT OF YOUR BED. BECAUSE LOOKS CAN BE DECEIVING AND YOU COULD BE LEFT FOR DEAD.

Chapter 22

My First Love Left Me Today

My first love left me on today for another girl that came his Way. He liked her talk and her walk. He liked the way she made him feel, even though he had a love that was sweet and real.

She had 3 babies in her hand, and one not born to understand, that in the midst of her deadly scheme she took what I knew was to be my dream.

A dream of goals and love that lasts, a dream of the present and not the past. A dream of hope and companionship, a dream of warm kisses on my Lip. A dream of fun and laughter all day, a dream of moving and making our own way, a dream of family and a happy day.

My first love left me on today, as he smiled and went his merry way. In the distance I saw a love fade. Then I made up my mind to love another one day. The time that was spent can never be replaced or erased. I can't go backward I must move on. I have a family, a place, a home.

God knew what He was doing when He said, "Just go your way." It left us both room to grow and pray. We might not have known right from wrong, but now we have no excuse, because we have both moved on.

I will choose to be your friend and nothing more. I will choose to forgive, let die and let go. I will choose to be happy and let you, too.

Deep down inside you are stuck in the past. You caught a glimpse of history and held on tight. Let it go for your sanity and your heart, so you will know when God sends you your beauty queen. God has someone special for you and it is not me. I just pray He opens your eyes to see that your soul mate will set you free.

MY FIRST LOVE LEFT ME ON TODAY, NOW HE'S BACK AND HE WANTS TO STAY. PICK UP WHERE HE LEFT OFF, BUT IT'S WAY TOO LATE…

Chapter 23

Flashback in Time.....

Do you remember yesterday? We stayed on the phone the whole day, talking about what we wanted to do, ignoring our stomachs as they growled at you.

Do you remember those long rides in the sunset, running through water, getting our feet wet?

Do you remember fussing at me and being mad, me feeling upset and being sad?

Do you remember all those letters that I use to write, you saying, "Wow! It don't take all that." Twenty-one pages you would read for days, and each day was a new letter, I was serious I had something good to say!

Do you remember looking high and low for me? Checking here and there for me? Asking all around for me? Not even having a number for me? Do you remember all those school days, where smiles were happy and went on for days?

Do you remember fighting for me, over me or about me? These were the days of the young in age to have good times, not care and play; but, when you take a flashback in time, you must be ready to remember the good and the bad, the happy and the sad...the hurt and all the pain.

We must remember what really happened to make this a part of our history. We do have history and lots I dare say, but something happened for it to fade away. Do you remember late night drives, holding each other while we joke and jive.

Do you remember leaving me, or me leaving you? The way we felt as we went our way, something inside just broke and fell.

Do you remember being all alone? Being told you just wanted to move on? That's me. I know that feeling & it's not good. Puppy Love gives you the Blues. I remember bits and pieces of our love, but you remember way too much. A flash back is just a memory but you are making it a lifestyle. It's a New Day.

My life is great! I have no worries or concerns. I am free. Then I get a Facebook request from a friend of old. Wow! How could this be? Where has he been? It's getting late, it 5 best 10.

I accept this request and we start to talk. Immediately I knew something was wrong, for to the past he has been holding on.

"Stop this nonsense," is what I said. "I have a family, a husband, kids and a maid. It's a new day for me you see. I have forgotten about the past and covered it up. Then you come along and dig it right up!

"How could this be, it's been so long? I think it's a trick from the enemy, to tear me up and hold me captive. Sin is secret, so you think, but Gods forgives and sets you straight.

"We can't live in the past, we have to forgive, move on, let it go and have a blast. Time is too short to hold on the extra.

"I told you I would be your friend, that should not be hard to understand. If we can't be friends then that's your loss.

"I want you to understand that I have a loving, caring, sweet, handsome, adorable, understanding, sexy man. I would not trade him for the world because he is the father of my girls.

"To open a spiritual gateway will lead me straight to hell and rock my family to NO prevail. I know right from wrong and I choose to do right. If I choose to do wrong then that is selfish on my part, and why would you want a woman that only thinks about her heart?

"IT'S A NEW DAY TODAY, FOR ME AND YOU, SO PRAY TO GOD AND HE WILL SHOW YOU JUST WHAT TO DO. HE WON'T GIVE YOU ANOTHER MAN'S WIFE, BECAUSE THAT IS NOT IN THE BOOK OF LIFE. HE WILL SEND YOU YOUR OWN, TO LOVE AND CHERISH AND MOVE YOU ON."

I Am Different by Design!

www.ingramcontent.com/pod-product-compliance
Lightning Source LLC
Chambersburg PA
CBHW051701090426
42736CB00013B/2476